benediction
for a
black swan

Tess Gallagher, excerpt from "Instructions to the Double" from *Midnight Lantern: New and Selected Poems.* Copyright © 1976 by Tess Gallagher. Reprinted with the permission of The Permissions Company, Inc. on behalf of Graywolf Press, Minneapolis, Minnesota, www.graywolfpress.org.

Brief quote from p. 53 from *Shadow Tag* by Louise Erdrich. Copyright (c) 2010 by Louise Erdrich. Reprinted by permission of HarperCollins Publishers.

Published 2015
Printed in the United States of America
ISBN: 978-1-63152-950-4
Library of Congress Control Number: 2015930468

Book design by Stacey Aaronson

For information, address:
She Writes Press
1563 Solano Ave #546
Berkeley, CA 94707

She Writes Press is a division of SparkPoint Studio, LLC.

benediction
for a
black swan

Mimi Zollars

SHE WRITES PRESS

table of contents

III.

IV.

for Fallon

"If you're a poet you do something beautiful. I mean you're supposed to leave something beautiful after you get off the page . . ."

— *Franny and Zooey*
J.D. Salinger

I.

"I would believe only in a God who could dance."

—FRIEDRICH NIETZSCHE

word   I write like a girl
unabashed   naked
dancer's body open   revealing

childhood formed
by the catholic church
ballets ache for perfection

I can still swag a tutu
recite the stations of the cross

from briny atlantic ocean
pure cold pacific deep
infused waters of hawaii
churning gulf   the dirty south

I write of requited   unrequited love
found and lost
how divine I am
and you —

light bright   eternal   darling
somebody's lover   ex lover   beloved

I write poems for you   holy water
prayer beads scattered   glittered
pillow of roses beneath my hips

seattle
london fog
afternoon
most beautiful man
hands full of
light
designs
a moon colored
dress
for her

for him
she becomes
a shimmering
goddess
swathed
in silk satin
smoking the
black tarry hash
he loves

he loves
young men
breaks her heart
creates
dresses
that worship
glimmering
skin

old hotel bar
drinking
sazeracs
elegant
blushing patrons
surreal
conversations

she loves
the effect
of bourbon
of him
of life
resembling
art

| josé louis rodríguez guerra

inside his beautifully lit studio
paintings adorn the walls
gessoed canvases await color
like young girls waking in early morning light

tarot cards scattered on the floor
small pile of silver pesitos beside
rosa y rojo candle burning down

josé louis rodríguez guerra
smells of vertivert and lime
thick sweet coffee   pink sugared crumbs
from a pan dulce

his paintings like dreams
where he creates and perceives the world
simultaneously

woman dressed as a man
family wedding portrait
white gown   black suits amid garden flowers
waxy green leaves

nude reclines
in paloma grey shadows
on ornately carved bed
breasts arcing with desire

at night he takes down his canvases
paints the walls behind
shimmering black birds in flight
gold dust falling onto broken glass

she knows because he has shown them to her

where do you sleep   she asks

the studio is devoid of furniture

never taking his eyes from her face
sweetly seductive hands
hover over the floor
where a mattress might be

she lifts the flimsy dress
it flutters away

he poses her
already making love
picks up the palette of glistening paints
stroking his brush on canvas

levitate me   her smile says
levitate my soul

enter a place of memory
tangerine door no longer squeaks
pink neon sign still glows   night descends on belltown

beautiful tim   diagnosed years ago
magnificent   radiant
despite curling smoke from his cigarette

euro-house blue eyes dance   svelte urban body
features chiseled within an inch of his life
tapering hands of an artist   cockatoo colors
stain his fingertips

comes out from behind the bar   arms open wide
clairvoyant smile   eyes lit
from that vast inexplicable place he resides

I was thinking about you   he says

it's been over twenty years

I was thinking about you all day

hugs me wonderful hard

and of course here you are

boyish voice exactly like him
bright orange shirt   striped dandy pants

silver key on a long looping chain

remember that party on the rooftop at 6th and union?

esmae showing him the keyhole tattoo
behind her ear
the skeleton key tattoo on his ankle

we both got them on the same day   we didn't plan it

how our lives used to be exactly that way

tells about getting a shave around midnight
from a gorgeous man in Istanbul
the last night of their trip
razor and strap   how erotic

shows me the sandals he bought
on the isle of lesbos   laughs

I have to wear them every day

finished his opus 17 years ago
ginormous canvas covered in paint
how it completed him
met his life's love that same night   he shrugs

I was just finished making art

inexplicable smile   he radiates loving kindness
exudes vision and peace

of course he does

he spends all day searching

in the market   beneath hot moroccan sun
parchment silhouette of a dancer   ink on body
set free   flies across the desert

a terrible place to lose one's way

shrouded man ambles past
apothecary bottles jangle
from a piece of driftwood
carried across his shoulders

imagines his lover's garden plunging towards the sea

old village woman walks by
painting in a gold frame   under her arm
a seascape perhaps
a still life of his heart

whenever a fairytale is told it becomes dark

archeologists   travelers   writers
drink champagne beneath desert stars
the best stories like light tattoos   on skin

the excessive love of anything
how dangerous it is

he remembers her naked
clothes on a red chair by the door
in love with ghosts   the broken piano playing

ghosts summoning the piano

considers the hollow
at the base of a woman's throat
the pulse   the holiness there

he spends all day searching
at night he wants to be found

lofty window of her studio
reflecting empty dawn
tiny bird skulls
cobalt wings
flower child beads strung
suspended in daylight

momentary   balance
an amends perhaps
for the cigarette she once put out
in a gloating vase of expensive flowers
at a Chihuly opening

that same night
she shattered the exquisite goblet
created with the aim of surviving
a single evening
unaware she had fulfilled its
destiny

she paints the scapulars
turquoise on calcified bone
sunlight tints the sacrum
color of geological stones

a form that serves no other function
than to alleviate regret

significance as a work of art
negligible
yet releases the essence of
the ideas she loves
everywhere

the sculpture
no longer pretends to be
unassuming
commands attention

precise edges   bone sharp
the sculpture embodied
begins to float

pink door   post alley
pass right by its secrets
pike place market   seattle
mystic city swathed in mist

interior   light from windows slants
dust motes dance a languid waltz
smell of sweet peas   rustic bread   espresso

yesterday   in this same place
a young woman in jay's wing dress
tattooed roses   thorns
rising from the bloom of her breast

worn cards drawn from a satin bag
embroidered with tree limbs   birds
star and sun   the lover's globe shaped world
water   fire   earth   air

small tributaries will flow into a shimmering stream
gathering light and velocity

what will you do to prepare   for what is ready   for you?

the psychic gathered her effects
cards   candle   vintage silk cloth
cut from the canopy of a hungarian circus
trailing china rain perfume

she orders a manhattan
cherry cold bourbon
angostura bitters on a sugar cube
elixir swirls and settles
sunset in a glass

early evening   the bar almost empty
la bohème lilting
trapeze from late night cabaret
hangs in captivating stillness
on the tiny stage

your life will open twice before its close

when the portal reveals itself   do not hesitate to step through

windows turn the color of violets
glasses clink   tables shine with silver settings
two young women at the bar   sip neon blue drinks
faces glow lavender in the *pink door* sign

I keep falling in love   one of the lavender lit girls says
I keep falling in love with everyone   everywhere

I see the strand colored man
feet dug into engraved hieroglyphs of the shore

blue eyes scan the sea
gem cut scarabs   wings spread   interrupted flight

filled with visions   a past I can never glean
those perfect foreign blooms gathered to his breast

smile   the color of a wedding gown
saccharina so sweet it disbelieves

he never says it was a mistake exactly
no one marched him down the aisle

poured liquor into his sanguine throat
placed vows in his mouth   strange and thick as licorice

he lights   *caro mio*
when I tell him I found a unicorn in venezia

how my camera captured a lightning storm
laguna veneta   fantastical as a dark painting by seurat

on the train to la spezia   elegant man from trieste
thought we were british because we spoke english so well

no noble blood in our veins   no schooling abroad
perhaps we simply enjoy being understood

he does not move
there on the restless edge of sea
colorful drops of my tales' rainbow glisten his eyes

the sarcophagus at villa borghese
guarded by dragons   enchanted purple hollyhocks

bent to the ground in exquisite genuflection
thistles like sentries under bright roman sky

my old sweetheart
smiles through high ancient dome

a temple to memory   basilican effulgence
dancing mosaics across his face

cannot untomb his feet from the sand
if he were to reach for me   he might come undone

like those heavy heads of statuary flanking il vittorio
tumbling off in the midst of a still afternoon

the view at riomaggiore   sucked the breath from me
how bare shoulders are too sexy for church

my siren's hands flow visions towards him
his eyes   the reflection of hurt

absorbing marital obligations
no longer searching for statues by bernini   everywhere

baroque musical fountains   theatrical arches
ancient obelisks

how much of love is removing spells

la magia del mar in my hands   cupping sweet
I reflect all of the light in his face back at him

beautiful lover   sexing magic
ghost forever unearthing pearls
from the georgia o'keeffe flower of me

no longer dying   realized perhaps
unlike hemingway   radiating sulphur
surprised by your sweetness
sugar cube mist   green tea of this city

all those words and poetry   however unintentional
amplified us over time
nude paintings still stir our souls
indelible ink of our veins

silken evening drops   black like fading pens
quickened by infatuation
and complicity

I no longer wear chanel lipstick
smudging red   deliberate worship
left behind in secret

how I loved being the girl
paint of picasso   blue dress
leonard cohen my muse
because I believed I could seduce him

nightscape of seattle
the desire of men
always some foreign doorway
bruising   tender and rough

my denuded swan lake thighs
essence of anaïs nin

how much I still hold dear
chartreuse glint   your eyes
conjuring a world where we can live

the tropic of somewhere

| benediction *for a* black swan

everything about the ballet is lovely except the hemlock

vintage dress cut low in back
bourbon   smoke from her gauloises cigarette

tender   bruising violet
erotic silhouette   in or out of costume

endless rehearsals   black lace tutu
bracelets made of rosary beads

thirty two fouettés en tournant
one hundred fifty three hail marys   in fifteen decades

dangling dark crucifix

adagio reaching towards its star
extending   crowning   discolored by pain

her ruthlessly romantic
view of the world   not uninformed

fierce passionate being
wild daughter   will you ever rest

II.

"And the day came when
the risk it took to remain
tight in a bud was more
painful than the risk it
took to blossom."

—ANAÏS NIN

rosary beads   a form of devotion   decades of
hail marys   our fathers   glory be
rosa   rosarium   rosary from the latin
rose gardens   the ones in mind
always shades of pink   sweetheart   ballet
cherry blossom   1963 valentine
frothy beverages with a sour fruity aftertaste
the effect alcoholics   adore

pink nothings   pink ladies   pink gin
rinse a cocktail glass with bitters
fill with london dry chilled
color of her sex   color of the chanel suit
jacqueline kennedy wore the day jack was assassinated
color of rose quartz broken open on the back porch
in 1973   and your first pair of pointe shoes

in the french catholic tradition
learn to fear your passions   sinful impulses
later   embrace them like pale petals
wild   precious   darlings —
pink monkey flowers   carnations   the vulva
heart shaped bulb of vestibule
amaryllis   narcissus   tulips

include the paintings of georgia o'keeffe
old women   their terrible smudging lipstick
snapshots of girls who are damaged
beautiful   because they are damaged

the only way to be saved in this world is to love
learn to love

I want warmth
heat lightning and beauty   huge
bouquets of roses   gathered from our garden

I want my young mother
in an old-fashioned bathing suit   smelling of baby oil
iodine   spoiling her children with shine

ocean breezes
salt and sun   a bonfire on the beach at night
to levitate a grown man from the sand

chanting a haunting rhythm
over and over   in elliptical dark

he is light as a feather   strong as a board

chanting as my daddy levitates eerily

wee children   powerful smiles
sure of supernatural aptitude in our little hands

I want summer
black and white photographs   my once
happy mother   orange kissed sisters

tired of darkness
cold hands   sky that lacks luster   if it does not
contain heat   I do not want to remember

I want the forever long days of childhood
lightning storms at twilight   electric fireflies

to smell that old ozone smell   magic spilling
from my warm skin onto my children

into their mouths   bright and wondrous looks
back from their starry eyes

you dream of roses often   growing   climbing
all over the house   shades of white   ivory   cream
not like a funeral   palest moonflowers
their lemony incandescence

dreams of baptismal gowns   wedding veils
the exact color of your first communion
shades of the dress you were married in

a wedding like the mad hatter's tea party
forsaken   wild without ceremony

you dream of roses   southern scented magnolias
purple cabbage heads bleeding out
enormous dahlias remembered
from another   sweeter life
well loved   well worn   unraveling

you dream the garden of your heart
lushly petaled flowers
vines smell like sex   like babies breathing

fantastic party beneath a willow tree
white lanterns glow opaque darkness
the chance you may get to love someone again

a heart cannot contain only darkness
things fall apart
begin with the smallest crack
light will find a way to seep back in

be still and remember who you are
beloved daughter of the universe
blooming from the inside out
breathe in   sweet fragile scent of answered prayers

| s h i s e i d o   r e d   *and*   g i n   *in*   h e r   t e a c u p

cherries split and bleeding   in the orange bowl
remembering the broken day   her head
smacked the wooden floor
silk kimono slid open   crimson poppy red
flushed against skin

you don't remember anything

not the pain or startled hurt
sudden indrawn breath   belief vanished
regret bloomed   chrysanthemum burst

irrevocable sunset spread   burning color
transcendent slant of sun   enough
to cast   pooling disbelief

don't say there is no veil
the mist always there

between still pond   dark mirror
endless soul filled night

see how you
no longer cast a shadow

flowing water
reflects your face
engraved by pain and love

ornate frame of willow
live oak trees
a temple to worship from

hold a stem in your mouth
carry a bowl of water

gather up   this armful of stars
no one else can see what you see

illusory isolation

souls who see through you
gazing at their perfect likeness

| *the* b e a u t i f u l   b r i d g e   d i d   f a l l

after louise erdrich

'*In every picture, at the end of his mother's hand,*
Stoney drew a stick with a little half-moon on the end of it …
The wine glass.
Irene was silent.
He thinks it's part of you …'
— shadow tag

notice the wineglasses   in every scene
include mysterious possibilities
the art of falling down   passing out
breaking in and out of windows

observing small superstitions
she began to drink every day
believing this strange vigilance
would somehow make her happy

covering her shadow
with tiny bottles of glittering gin

she kept forgetting
the soul is visible
the soul is visionary and fearless

she did not love him anymore
she quit sleeping with him

I want you to leave   he said

she saw white   ceruse   lead carbonate
dead poisonous and insanely pure

she went mercurial overnight

I cannot stand him

she began drinking wine like water
though he was no longer there
to refill her glass

I'd better fade away   she would reason

night   after night   after night

she could smell a fragrance
not flowery but negligent
some exotic emotion linked to pain

folding origami paper
the dove   birds of peace

she kept wishing he would die

in the end
trying to take her own life was not wrong
something had to happen

crack like a shattered mirror
on the surface of a sunless sea

miraculous champagne
filigreed label   ornate and broken
she awakened to the presence
of a strange grace
even cynics might call love

love is a mean story   cut glass cuts
the wall that separates   high as china

they say discomfort is the heart of expansion

I say   leave me alone

darjeeling girl   sweet pea   honey bee
blue-eyed baby

no one ever said being a mother could kill you

even the flowers in the garden
turn away

tea roses riveted in terror
tiny thorns   not enough protection
release mists of fright into summer sweet air

any part of a lily could do in the cat

a mouthful of blossoms
seeds   bulb   leaf   petal
inviting mild discomfort   or death

she wishes I would die

golloping all the birthday cake herself
gleefully mincing on my grave
wearing the mad hatter's hat

topped with lighted candles   lit
lavender   yellow   orange   blue
joyously aflame

I would be manageable as dirt
smolder   ashes   sundered
unable to keep her
drowning in the reflecting pond

tending the palma christi
most poisonous plant in the world
I will remind her
the end has already happened   twice

spiky green conicals
poofed silky carnelian
silly as the grinch's christmas tree

your pony in the pasture
those oleander   you knew he was too smart to eat

still dangerous   dead   like   that

I'm not waiting up for you
deadheading pinks   bedraggled   ruffling grey
rumpled   weary

dolls eyes   winter cherry
heart of sweet jesus

what doesn't kill you   I say

who turns bitterness to love?
who changes the poisonous snake around your neck to pearls?
— rumi

I come away from her tarnished
ring of green around overwrought wrists
as if I have been wearing nickel bracelets
disguised as silver

unable to give thanks and praise
say the glory be
twine my hands in onyx beads
alone and apart

bow my head until catharsis ordains a way
smooth thorny spines coated in black wax
where deep purple flowers
come undone

I wash my dark sister from my hands
scent of lacquered black birds   juniper berries
flowing down copper drain

anoint my wrists and throat with henna
glance in the oval mirror   distressed at the edges

I wait until I recognize my face
violet marks beneath my eyes
begin to fade

goodness comes to nest in my heart
like a terrible   winding snake

I have buried my mean-spiritedness
beneath a moss covered rock
beneath this fast moving stream

I intend for it to stay there
as I drag my fingers
along the edges of your heart

seeking the place
where you would not
cherish me   despite eons

of broken down I love yous

somewhere
white narcissus blooms
under a tall spruce tree

rays slant through dense clouds
through the undamaged canopy
of lush layered green

cold water rushes by

shaken to receive the bouquet   and how to
banish the roses   without pricking her fingers

dangerous elemental reactions   alchemical backlash
blood droplets altering the course of destiny

she clasps the stems to her breast
the flowers   mostly cream and pink   turn red

when beheading darlings
you must be ruthless   lest it cause more suffering

finishing him off then becomes an act of mercy
she enters his soul   through voluptuous loathing

sweat turning fragrant as cocoa   dark
scorched aroma

the cold clear night   obeying a higher behest
throws her out   naked   iridescent   trembling

finally detached from him   her being dissolves
returns as something perfumed   aspiced   sensuous

scent of rocks and thorns   soil and figs
the bouquet of roses   utterly deconstructed

becalmed   close to midnight
children plunge into jewel green water
limestone banks lined with haunted mansion trees
bald cypress and pecan

new leaves filagreed against the night
huge passover moon encircled by nebula
the color of dragonfly wings

undisturbed river   deep and pure
not so cold it will suck the breath out of you
fresh   exhilarating   clean

you're not going to let them swim in the dark

firelight gleams
she pulls down long gypsy sleeves
covers the rings on her fingers
too many   perhaps

touches the center of her heart
my darlings   my wilder beings

lifts her chin
the children are carnival silhouettes
beneath proscenium arch of trees

capable of great good magic
enchantment descends   fearless   powerful
the kind of night that enlarges you from inside out

she hopes they will steal a cigar
from the charismatic man   with the lovely hands
hopes they smoke it because they feel untamed and free
cartwheeling across the milky way

later   when they fall asleep
damp hair and clothes tangled
full of light   gypsum traces drying on their skin

how it never occurs to her   to tell them no

you all have these secret lives

side by side
draped across the wicker divan
their bodies paisleyed with salt
from swimming in the gulf all afternoon

you know I love you

the daughter lifts sparkling water
drinks from the glass
before passing it to her mother

why do you do that

yours tastes better   always

the daughter's finger traces
a long scar on her mother's throat

you can hardly see it now

moonflower vines cling to weathered rails
searching for higher vistas

do you think I needed surgery
because I was hanged in a past life

ghastly   but anything is possible

the fragrance from her mother's body
spicy   reminiscent of exotic lilies
behind pink stucco walls

it wasn't always like this

when she was drinking it was much darker
a bitter exhausted scent
the daughter could hate her for

she became a mystery
the children were incapable of solving
distressing   terrible in her destruction

the headiness of so many fragrant blossoms
nicotinia   gardenia   jasmine
night blooming clematis   almost overwhelming

it isn't difficult to forgive a woman who made amends
planting hundreds of deliberate white flowers
all over   everywhere

it's only interesting you used to drink
now you have managed to stop

darkness settles   night descends
enfolding the small island where they live

you have such incredible strength
you will always know what to do

lit up at the heart of the universe
both of them sun tired   content

the daughter smiles   one long arm
like a willowy stem
reaches to caress her mother's face

the sudden gratitude for her changing

so   tell me darling
would you have preferred the ordinary

they know the botanical names for love
gunpowder blue edges
funeral whites gathered at the centers

holy   holy   holy

lowering myself on tentative silk
into the misty room of thrones
trailing cigarette smoke   damp plummeting dove

the commencement of fidelity
poofs of flight feathers billowing   caught
in a high dispersing wind

december when our island is cold or mud

holy   holy   holy

the glass sharp version of me disappearing
distilled droplets gathering condensation
in the swell of a sugar spoon

compelled by emblematic bursts of sentiment
the kings   crowns tipped sideways
no longer suffering from luminous dipsomania

blue hymnals   hazy room
echoing the sound of dark spirituals
hand clapping   foot stomping

a complete untruth
as darkness moved slowly through and away from me

holy   holy   holy

sipping promises like soul water
swimming with sober men
steeped men who never forget the taste of gun oil

passionate men   their self effacement
eventually compelling my utter devotion

holy   holy   holy

flung to the far edges of soiled grey
vortices converge at the heart of me

bloodless bird regathering   spiritus sanctus
canting the latin names for flowers

conjugating the verb
amō   amāre   amāvī   amātus

holy   holy   holy

prone on a large flat rock
beside a slate pool
taste of mineral   stone   loam

blood the source of memory
powerful   red as crushed gemstones
once imbued in paintings

no one really wants to keep secrets
especially the dead

rare shimmer
becoming more distinct

imagines she is nowhere
anywhere that has no name

scent of willow sap
moss crushed beneath a careless foot
fallen oak leaves

the palimpsest on her skin
traces of lines   become discernible

effacing earlier drawings
green lion   anjou peacock

birds alight in the cover of trees
charcoal blackbirds rimmed in ink

panes of light
slant across the vellum of her body

they have been waiting a long time for her

readiness flows
toward the deep end of the stream
hardly a virgin on this altar

hollows at the base of her spine
collect condensation

a bowl filled with stones
removed from her pockets
absorbing wave and particle

in bone deep quiet they call to her

the compass tracings
surface on her skin

III.

"At the end of his life,
Freud admitted his
understanding of the
female psyche was
limited. If you want to
know more about the
nature of femininity, you
will have to consult the
poets."

—*MASTERS OF SEX*
SEASON I, EPISODE VI

focus intently on the eyes
black and white irises
nine ravens alight in my tree
rustling leaves sound like rain
one flies away

clock chimes eight and gloaming

birds build nests in circles
symbol of infinity
distracted by shine
the love scenes   the glamour
wedding ring glittering its beak

I am happy it was you

jazz   bass   cello   swell in the distance
the birds are not bereft
are not having wine before dinner
pinot noir   fragile heartbreak grapes

grateful for this darkness
lustrous purple black mantle
blue ebony feather
clock face hangs around my neck
the promise of eternity

take up this vision
arms trained to slow   smooth   adage
sway your hips
imagine kissing someone properly
experience is an asset

drape yourself around the night

| c e r u l e a n   b l u e   *and*   I   d r e a m

nightfall flows through my veins
throbs my throat

the citrus trees in your yard
have more fruit than ever   ripened by apricot sun

evening drops releasing fragrant blush
sharp lemon   perfumed kaffir lime

entering your house I sense something foreign   exotic
moon soaked shutters open to a courtyard
ancient drums   tremolos of africa

blood red walls like the inside of a pomegranate
enclose   pink guava   wisteria   fig

holding a lit cone of incense
in your palm   the rapturous heart of this

they say I am a writer
lavish tendrils   secret imprints   lush   edgy

our shoulders brush
sparking meteor showers of syringa blooms
cascades fall   syrup sweet

I see you are a man who falls in love easily
pause   drift   steady
silver bangles harp to my wrists

black tree trunk gnarled and twisting
leaves dapple your face with magic green

are we really   you say
so close I can taste your breath

recalling beautiful lost words no one uses
nigrescence   obsecration   refulgence

words I will never say out loud

calmed by well water rising toward cerulean
we gather into one another

I am a poet and I dream
a prayer answered exquisitely

high above   bright burning venus
anchors us to this galaxy

birds of paradise flying
over fields of honeydew
lit by sulphur torches
marrakech ahead on
infinite curve of horizon

behind city walls
mint leaves   jasmine   hibiscus
worship inside dented copper teapots

sultry night air hung with music
strange exotic tongues
smell of sex lingering in cups of tea
everyone seems to leave behind

darkness deepens
longs for one mean kiss
and then the taste of him
green salted lime

silver loop of earring
caught between his teeth
lost in her wild sea

beyond the land of god
galaxies shiver into existence
the universe delights in
its own delirious expansion

the lovers leave traces
etched into the night

preternatural darkness
moonlight woven with sterling strands

conjured intermingling
the genius of playing your mind

arms like swans unfolding
camisole slips off
influencing the cover of night

skirt lifted   pale thighs   bare breasts
seek to reflect light

duet fills the cadenced room
white field of body blossoms

ankles wrapped in otherworldly ribbons
pink satin   delicate tarsals
blood anoints   veins   capillaries   arteries

divan the color of ash
velvet pillows   gossamer as old souls

windows open wide
as winter waves flow to shore

opera written in seraphic ink
flushes the color of desire

bones in the shape of a V   inviolate
respond to the unblooming   yield

lush opening
as the moon becomes the dancer

is this the rapture you remember

holy triumvirate
love   sexing   magic

rhythmic behind closed eyes
the ambient garden of your name

wearing a crown of roses
having transposed the hedge of thorns

primordial song born of water
remember your true religion

he finds and lights
the candles
silken prayer
to her skin

flickering flames
trellis umbrage
on her body
against
lush garnet cushions

intuitive breath
venerating
the long
shadowed length
of her

languid night
struck
by forbidden stars
essence
of devotion

| all I hear back is I love you   I love you

if anyone asks you how the perfect satisfaction
of all our sexual wanting will look
lift your face and say   like this
— rumi

frail membrane tearing away
how it would feel to cleave a soul
from its bodily casing

so sheer and fragile
so all everywhere and tenacious

rend in delicate fabric
more tenuous than a silk moth wing

how did it come to this

becalmed river   just after the bend
sun begins to rise
reflecting live oak and alder   stricken willow

spun web caught   bewildered
unable to find its reflection on water

supine along the river's edge
transparent trees drip spanish moss
amid dead limbs   rotting flowers

tears seep from the corners of my eyes
intense flare burns them into my skin

how did it come to this

washing leaves from the branches of my hair
the clairvoyant was right   in the end
he is alone inside the circumference of himself

the whole purpose of love is drowning
to dissolve   become more

surrounded by a quiet so intense
it creates ripples on the water
ever expanding   dissipating
from the stone dropped in the center of my being

this time I have left a garden behind
not trampled or damaging or destructive

beds of perennials   love and laurel
hollyhock   the absence of hemlock
roses tinged red at their throats

stillness settles   a place of prayer perhaps
moisture begins collecting
in the basins of my collarbones

nothing stays the same

peonies like planets hang from thin stalks
african jasmine   shoulder blades like wishbones
beneath sage charmeuse

we have mortared and limed bones of our past
poured final bottles of wine back into this earth
fragrant with loss   a failure to love

I have searched the mounds gravely
unearthed our darkness
fears only love can reform
frail chalice of sea flowers   fierce remorse

I am leaving a moss framed mirror
resemblance of druid worship
my breasts bound in white moonbeam cloth

hands tangled in adulation   dirt beneath my nails
as we lie on a bed of earth   lush and loamy
the carpals of your hands crushing
sharp stones beneath

we are not lost

from this long night until morning
stay   worshipping
cupping into your nearness
hipbones sculpted and impeccable

scraped cuts like petals
feet covered in hennaed mud
designs ancient and precise

peeling my body away
my imprint in the sacred raiment of your skin

| give me *a* dark room
and I will give you *an* adulteress

you are lying in bed
at the other end of the long universe
beside your wife   not touching

I luxuriate
having avoided another maze of sundays
unetched palms of my hands
smooth as the inside of my soul

wild hair unleashed
the dark sea of this room
sybarite curtains glow

I feel your desire
other   lover   familiar

intense complicity
fraught with danger
this potent violet evening

passion seeks its level
in my poet's heart
longs to be immortalized

be afraid

unaware
she has taken a piece of his raptured heart
torn her portion of thrall
and devoured it without mercy
leaves a void of desolation
washes it down   red and lusty as blood

places
wooden bowl of vertebrae on the table
deadly   white   strung with gypsy bells
the taste of salted limestone
from an orchard shadowed by fear

polaroid lenses of her glasses   darken in the sun
wailing wall   funeral scraps   endless devotions
damp smokey offerings
bones of her scapula observant and drawn

psalms beneath her irreverent blue dress
fragrant and forbidden   desire
so intense it leaves her breathless
bare feet skimming dust   heavy skirts lifted
sound of a thousand bohemian violins   in the wind

red juice so dark it's almost purple
stains fingertips pink like sex

where exactly is the soul

her lover's head buried
devout at her breasts
japanese silk falls open
scarlet flowering peony

where is it not   you say

heart of the afternoon
spills like sunshine across the bed
cabaret colored light through carnelian

a bit overwritten   don't you think

limbs intimately entwine
bird on the sill
tips one wing toward the east
the other toward the west

long slow silence ensues
ravishing her completely
carnal to the point of smoldering

buddha pass the bowl of cherries please

in the deep end of the pool
men observant from afar
my famous breasts
float lightly above the water

I am aware but do not care
having left all censure behind

the furthermost   expansive
version of me
slips itself on   swirling raiment
of particle and light

I find their use of latin names for flowers
voluptuous   *passiflora incarnata*
nymphea odorata
fragrant white water lilies

yucca gloriosa
ghosts in the graveyard
creamy flowers   stark crosses
float like apparitions

I thrill to their nearness
hope they will not notice
my spellbound body
try to rescue me

I conjure you now   anytime I wish
your face stirring desire
sudden profound awareness
of my presence

the trees draw closer
fern green fronds mirrored on water
undergo enchantment

I nudge the pool with my hands
unassertive   I swear
intrigued by the promise of allowing

I imagine signing autographs
india ink on beetle wings
the sound of laughter

realizing my soul's exact desire
and the beguilement of men

IV.

"Au milieu de l'hiver, j'ai
découvert en moi un
invincible été."

—ALBERT CAMUS

| b e n e d i c t i o n   m a r k   m o r r i s

life exists in the arc between two deaths
in the fall and the recovery
— doris humphrey

dance when you're broken open
— rumi

slipping my soul   into the soul
of my nineteen year old self

tossing you —
wild darling   the exuberant bouquet
universe lit up as your stage

grey tulle ring of saturn
orbiting your star

vibrant with tension
the ballet's arc of perfection
breath   lung   muscle   tendon

nine pm rehearsal call
k2 lager   his clove cigarettes

one two three   two two three

black swan eyes   alabaster skin
slash of red lipstick
leave your mind backstage

serpentine whisper   snaking your throat   *darling*
I hope you don't make love like you dance
you're fucking boring

sweat droplets   blood petaling black satin
back carved by pain and grace

flaming queen   maniacal maestro
famous kohl eyes   his famous dark impulses

one two three   two two three

in full flight   the waltz of shame
down vacant streets   freezing winter rain

nightclub   ecstasy   bathroom sex
dancing with gods and daemons
bourbon straight   fucked up love medicine

one two three   two two three

strike a sinuous pose —
slithering   shimmering   dance

undress for him
pray for him   those endless relentless mirrors
porcelain hipbones   les sylphides thighs

you burned for him   let him burn for you

stage lights flood
black sequins explode   dark glittering dove

one two three   two two three

lifted like an olive branch
my sadistic queen   my liege

fuck you   *fuck yeah*   dance

falling asleep   immaculate cold linen sheets
black cashmere sweater
orchidaceous labellum
showy   complex   psyche
leg warmers lengthen   pivot over knee

earlier
a decision   this matter of casting spells
tossing silver coins   mandalas
into the flowing fountain   no one else can see

doors   windows   flung wide
symphony no 7   movement 2   beethoven
rhapsodic   circular
wind sweeping corners   tresses wild

the declaration   *there is room for more love here*

muse   poet   white witch
lucid in the realm of creation

later   calm restored
powerful magic let loose
removes his hands from your waist

the universe   bemused   tosses him out
declaring its dominion

how the once worshipped becomes estranged

midnight
sybarite   feline purring   absolute darkness
a voice compelling

you are   I am

time lengthens   curving on itself

how much of change is simply letting go

awakening
too cold for any goddess to bathe in the sea
winter white sand
pillared grey green water   hueless temple

breasts wrapped in solstice cloth
protecting   lungs   ribs   brilliant red heart
discards the gown of light

begins unraveling   his precise fit like a glove soul
ribboning skin   raw   sacrificial
unbinding   flesh   mineral   blood

breathless   shimmering pain
pulling him out by the roots
majestic   ancient as the tree of life

whites out
returns to the immaculate field of poppies

strange flowers   lithographs   appear in the sand
precise   miraculous

chorus from delibes' lakmé
purloined by rushing waves   rushes in

expansive glossy green rituals
behind indigo eyes

foreign rooms   perfumed threads
billowing curtains
ribbons of kimono purple

rosettes gilded in moroccan blue
bullfighters   red silk walls
scent of earth   sun also rises   orange

daring swoon-blooded sex
love in the terrain of the bull

all relationships are eternal
times you must draw blood

beasts graze inside your ribcage
fierce   drumbeating   aorta

dark continent   boundaries
white arabians pounding hooves
racing turquoise shores

you   so damn beautiful

thrust the sword between shoulder blades
an elegant death

infatuation rushing in   delirious birds
not of this earth   materialize in live oak tree
spectral silhouettes   ink stained night

you appear outside my window
mingling moon beam   juniper soap

those rough   hidden edges
last time I cut my hand
tea-bud blood drops staining floorboards

pain is a venerated form of awakening
yours not mine

slip inside the door   compressed embrace
slipping through dark portal of your blood stream

you must change your life

my presence creates a ripple
not magic exactly   effortless
slide into another version of existence

long fingers find silver buttons
glittering along knobs of spine
down the back of my dress

press hard against the wall
mellifluous   maleficence   a delicate balance

snaking tree blooms
black beneath watermarked silk

upended bare limbs
etiolated flowers   pale from lack of light
roots delve deep into my mind

I appreciate a man who knows exactly
where he wants to begin
sinking mouth to throat   hikes up the dress

outside   other worldly birds   night trill
frail bones beneath ruthless wings

entwining limbs   entangling
a billion shards of obsidian   shatter

scatter at breathtaking speed
reassemble precisely   sanctified

I slip back inside my own blood
you fade into saturated night

trailing the cusp of dawn
anticipating the next strange layer
a pleasure not to sleep

the ghostly birds and I take flight

| epilogue

light is a wave when you care but are uncertain
light is a particle when you are certain you don't care
that's heisenberg uncertainty princi-poetry   baby
— mark crawford

you don't need a lover sweetheart   you need a champion

dancers' bodies   both
subtle   sublime
despite moons of moons gone by

blithe in their nudity   compass window
reflects accolades from on high

his first words to her
at the ballet barre   too close   mouth to nape

you smell like sex

quickening blush
thousand petaled lotus   deep pinking   true

thralls to the close of him   always
sutra scented coitus
the gods bestowed them extravagant grace

spoons into her silken ions   folded wings   blades

you still smell like sex   baby

93

attention seeking palomas
his mathematician hands   brilliant sorcerer
indulges each breast

purrs the back of her ear

you're fine ageless star carbon

hands slow circle   snaking
slake abdomen to hips
infra-red odyssey

always surprised by what longs to be said —

my ex-husband was a neutron star

collapsing stars spin too fast
powerful and insanely dense
pulling everything into their orbit

I had trouble breaking free   drinking helped

turning her face to his   considers her mouth

when I finally quit hating him   I became light
I had no mass   I was easily bent by gravity

leaded glass   so old it has warped   reflects
dim interior

when I quit drinking   I became a rainbow

he moves on top of her   girding her to earth
aligning his body to hers   precisely

intense   weighted by the gravity of long affection

light is so strange   there is really nothing to it

rumpled sheets   white cotton sanctuary

I do not miss your darkness
I loved the taste of you   bourbon and cigarettes

prises his body away   lifts her in his arms
fireflies of starlight trail across the room

I gave up whiskey and duality   I am becoming pure love

you are impossibly light

positions her on the silk velvet divan
worn silvery threads   antique indigo

I barely exist

arranges satin pillows beneath her hips
studies the physical properties   the phenomena
fingertips   trace points of shimmer

may I kiss you there   lover

his impeccable manners
permission   permission   permission

don't look at me

pauses   lingering

are you looking

I am not

I'm an unobserved particle   I'm only hypothetical

slow serpentine trailing down

you are always observed   you always exist

considers stillness   initiation
embraces the surrendering

who is observing us then

shuddering sigh
brilliant   sutra   sublime

as above   so below   baby

the stillness of the sea
where everything is possible

distance   if we fall into it
where everything is possible

the secret you never tell and don't tell
and don't

who am I to be unafraid

my finished withs shudder into the sea
december   when I did not manage a way out of my life
december   when I ended an overlong affair
december   when love found you

you don't tell because no one believes you anyway

the lover inside your bedroom
though you are thousands of miles apart

the secret you tell and tell

there is no tangible distance
only the illusory field of perception

bumping into heartbeats
spherical bubbles that travel at the speed of light

one hundred eighty six thousand
three hundred miles per second

swimming in a sea of them
immersed in one another's expanding heart beats

the blur of wings vanishing
the blur of wings emerging

the stillness of the sea continues

so when you finally lay me down
I can swim into you

the stillness
where everything is possible

when we fall into it

tell me about the one who is coming

trust the journey
the light will become lapis like a candle burning

incarnation pink   smiling lips
white spun sugar bouquet

surrender   you will remember how

carousel ride
mythical creatures   winged horses   mermaids
mural of clouds

you must believe in the flow of happiness

vision becomes
light through silhouette of stars
pricked into the galaxy of a tent

henna flower and myrrh dreams

oasis sparkling
spilling from your hands
into his shining eyes

not knowing why it makes you happy

| let someone else describe sacred

surrender sensual mind

psyche longs for that one kiss
seductive   intuitive   surprising
succumbs to scent of verbena
along the coastal strand

prays for you   prays for me

afternoon of long slanting light
birdsong breaks along the shore
swirling grey green rosaline

foam colored hem of my dress
drenched in love
recedes   leaving room to breathe

leafing climbs weathered veranda
petals from the purple winecup
in expressive french
open to the sun
entwine bright sky with seaglass sea

finds you   finds me

how could I have prepared for this
breath becomes sacred
includes the flower of salt
and the soul of blue

| it's not every day *the* world
arranges itself *into a* poem *for* you

I dreamed you
I wished for your existence

if I love you it is because I have no choice
you were fierce poems I wrote —

after existential strip tease
cruelly brought me to my knees
bruising bones   broken wishbone   ashes   ashes

the universe unbuttoned itself
before I ever saw   then kissed   wanted
to lick your face

lucid uncanny awareness

thinking back to the ritual
beethoven's 7th   keening   clearing wind
the invocation — there is room for more love here

waiting days for the full moon
naked   shivery   for once casting the spell exactly
precise words   birchbark ink

burying the crystal   deep island sand
cactus flowers and suckled honey
the steps leading to my front door

holding my inner world aloft
winter undressed for us   blustery   raw
I knew when I said yes   it would be irrevocable

my house the color of intimacy
loosened   exhaling stars

capturing the precise moment
the unknown shivered into existence

I will embrace your gilded darkness
kiss your perfect dangerous mouth

allow your hands to my waist   slowly   slowly

I love you my love   come home

experiencing the mind of god
brilliant   infinite   hyacinth

ink rushing through veins
a fortune told in tea leaves
damp lotus flower on your skin

the design so universal
it must be love

I have borrowed
your fearlessness
cloaked in lush eroticism

blue velvet voice
fierce heart encompassing
the edges of provocative

holding a sceptered thistle
blackbird tucked behind my ear
blade at ready in its wing
in case I am not well received

resplendent and bereft of dress
arabesques of songbirds   from my hips
laden with rough cut words
love with a burnished grace

in my mind I lean into you
vulnerable   flawless   intriguing
as the starling murmuration
from my lips

you want what I have

the mockingbird is singing
voice contains seductive truth
miraculous dance from the vortex
laced with shards of glass

author's notes

benediction   mark morris is for Jennifer Mizel and the akashic muses.

bleeding edge is for Elisa Tobia.

lost is dedicated to Clark Waters.

seattle was our paris is for Mark Harlow.

Albert Camus quote, "Au milieu de l'hiver, j'ai découvert en moi un invincible été": translates to, "In the depths of winter, I discovered there was in me an invincible summer."

bleeding edge note: A starling murmuration is the ariel dance birds perform while flocking.

acknowledgments

Beyond appreciation to Ruth Asher and Ruby Peru Stell for endless edits and endless love. And to Brooke Warner for believing in my work. Names that make me shimmer: Fallon, Ryan and Hailey, Aimee Larson, Jeffory Ramsey, Denise Morrison, and Pascal Sapparrart.

about the author

photo credit: Theresa Coppock

MIMI ZOLLARS was raised on both coasts of the United States and currently resides on a small island off the Texas coast with her three children and beloved frenchman. Raised in the Catholic church and the ballet, her ruthlessly romantic view of the world is not uninformed.

Zollars attended the University of Washington, where she studied creative writing and dance.

SELECTED TITLES FROM SHE WRITES PRESS

She Writes Press is an independent publishing company founded to serve women writers everywhere. Visit us at www.shewritespress.com.

The Geometry of Love by Jessica Levine. $16.95, 978-1-938314-62-9. Torn between her need for stability and her desire for independence, an aspiring poet grapples with questions of artistic inspiration, erotic love, and infidelity.

Beautiful Garbage by Jill DiDonato. $16.95, 978-1-938314-01-8. Talented but troubled young artist Jodi Plum leaves suburbia for the excitement of the city—and is soon swept up in the sexual politics and downtown art scene of 1980s New York.

Cleans Up Nicely by Linda Dahl. $16.95, 978-1-938314-38-4. The story of one gifted young woman's path from self-destruction to self-knowledge, set in mid-1970s Manhattan.

Play for Me by Céline Keating. $16.95, 978-1-63152-972-6. Middle-aged Lily impulsively joins a touring folk-rock band, leaving her job and marriage behind in an attempt to find a second chance at life, passion, and art.

Bittersweet Manor by Tory McCagg. $16.95, 978-1-938314-56-8. A chronicle of three generations of love, manipulation, entitlement, and disappointed expectations in an upper-middle class New England family.

Stella Rose by Tammy Flanders Hetrick. $16.95, 978-1-63152-921-4. When her dying best friend asks her to take care of her sixteen-year-old daughter, Abby says yes—but as she grapples with raising a grieving teenager, she realizes she didn't know her best friend as well as she thought she did.

9 781631 529504